Sets ir

Contents

Contents	Page
Shells	2-3
Leaves	4-5
Flowers	6-7
Grass	8-9
Sticks	10-11
Stones	12-13
Feathers	14-15
Seeds	16

written by Julie Ellis
photographs by Claire Watkins

Some children got some big shells and some round shells.

They made a set of big, round shells.

They got some oval leaves
and some yellow leaves.

4

They made a set of oval, yellow leaves.

They found some little flowers
and some red flowers.

They made a set of little, red flowers.

They got some long grass
and some brown grass.

They made a set of long, brown grass.

They found some short sticks
and some white sticks.

They made a set of short, white sticks.

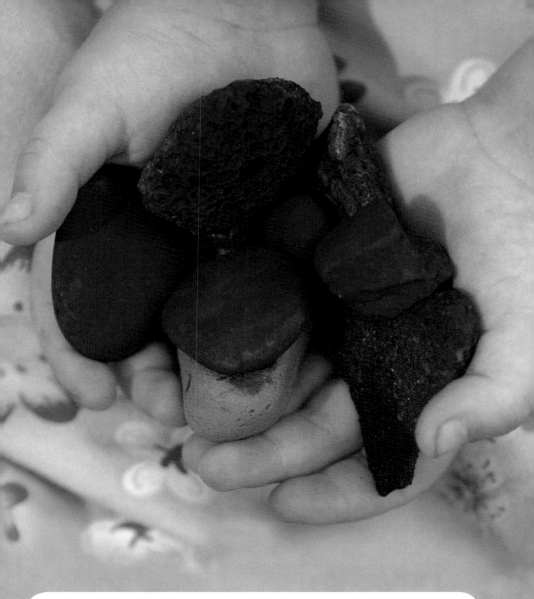

They got some flat stones
and some black stones.

They made a set of flat, black stones.

They found some pretty feathers and some blue feathers.

They made a set of pretty, blue feathers.

They found some seeds.
How will they make some
sets of seeds?